SEX
MASTERS
THE ULTIMATE CHALLENGE

SEX MASTERS

THE ULTIMATE CHALLENGE

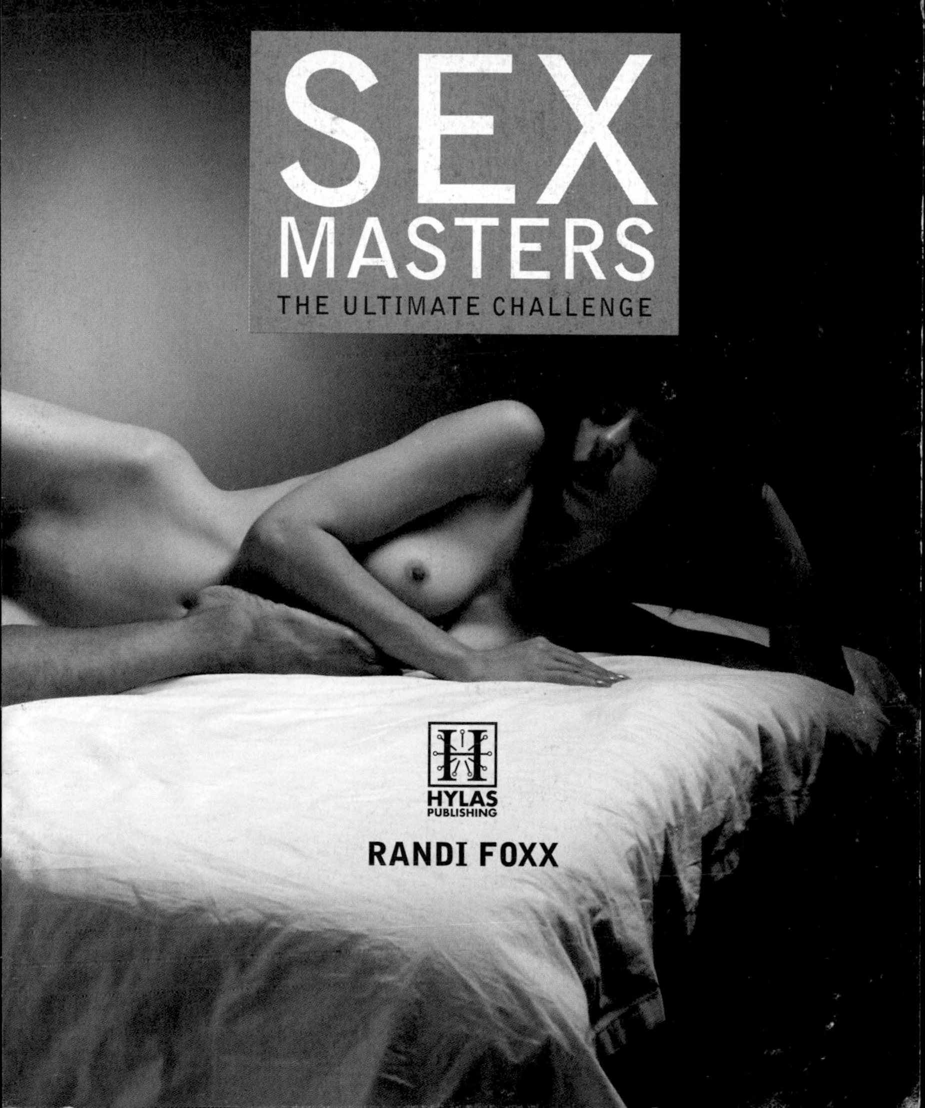

HYLAS PUBLISHING

RANDI FOXX

HYLAS

Hylas Publishing
129 Main Street, Suite C
Irvington, New York 10533
www.hylaspublishing.com

Hylas Publishing
Publisher: Sean Moore
Publishing Director: Karen Prince
Art Director: Gus Yoo
Editors: Ward Calhoun, Marisa Iallonardo
Assistant Editor: Kristin Maffei
Photographer: Robert Wright

ISBN-10: 1-59258-255-9
ISBN-13: 978-1-59258-255-6

Library of Congress Cataloging-in-Publication Data

Foxx, Randi.
Sex masters : the ultimate challenge / Randi Foxx. — 1st American ed. p. cm.
ISBN-13: 978-1-59258-255-6
1. Sex instruction. 2. Sex. I. Title.
HQ31.F784 2006
613.9'6—dc22
2006026309

Printed and bound in Singapore
Distributed in the U.S. by Publishers Group West
Distributed in Canada by Publishers Group Canada
First American Edition published in 2006

1 2 3 4 5 6 7 8 9 10

Contents

Checklist

Refresher Checklist

They say that nothing succeeds like success, and successful sex is a joy! This quick refresher checklist lets you relive the delicious and slightly more accessible positions of *Sex 101* and *Advanced Sex* and whets the appetite for more savory and sensational sexploits! So catch up and catch your breath and continue exploring and enjoying.

1 Straight-Edge Sex A

2 Foot Rub with Rhythm

3 Straight-Edge Sex B

4 Always by Your Sides

5 Pig in a Blanket

6 The Penitent Forgiven

7 The Awakening

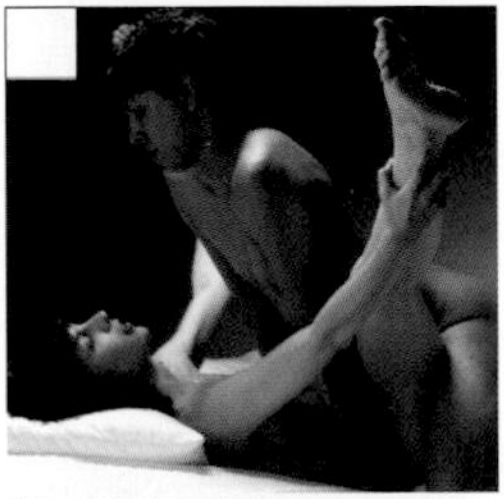

8 The Piked Awakening

9 Inner Awakening

10 Scissors

11 Splitting of a Bamboo

12 Hammerhead

13 Jackknifed Splits

14 Lateral Jackknifed Splits

15 Climbing Ivy

16 Inverted Wheelbarrow

17 The Crab

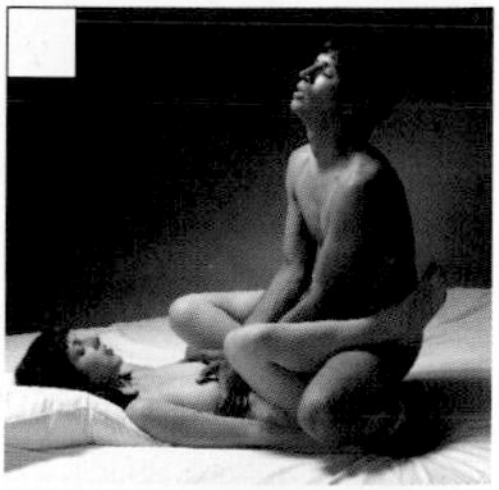

18 The Wrapped Crab

19 The Open Crab

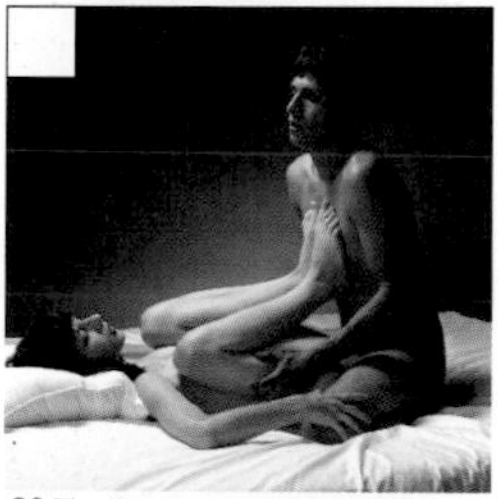

20 The Press

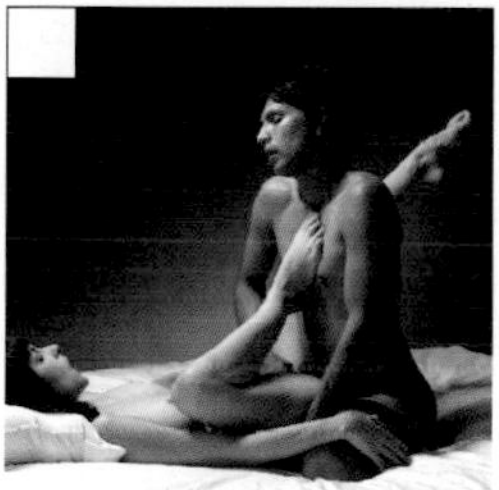

21 The Bicycle

22 Side-to-Side Press

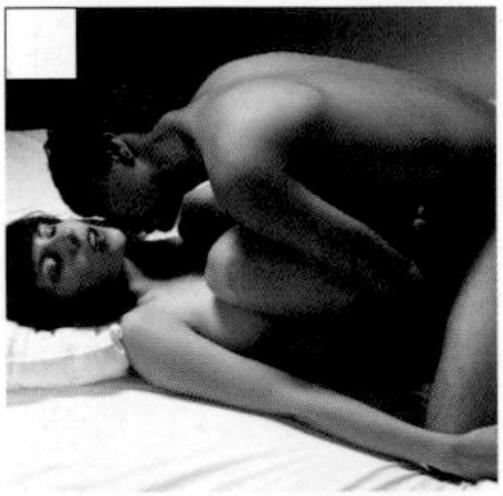

23 Half Lotus

24 Full Lotus

25 Wife of Indra

26 Kneel and Extend

27 Lateral Kneel and Extend

28 Kneel and Push Back

29 Side-to-Side Kneel and Extend

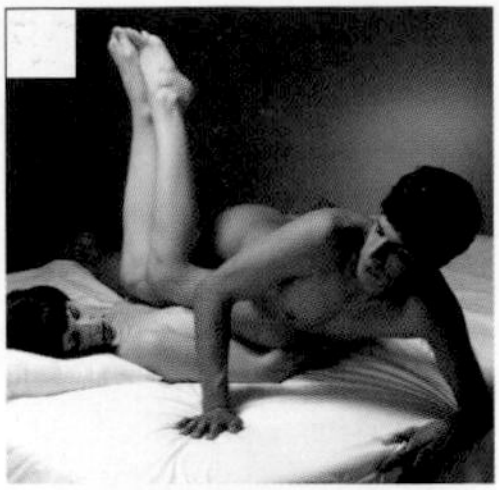

30 Surf's Up

31 Pelvic Thrust

32 Pelvic Lap Dance

33 Locked Lap Dance

34 Kama's Wheel

35 Reclining Kama's Wheel

36 Snake Trap

37 Full Reclining Snake Trap

38 The Neverending Hug

39 Paired Feet

40 "X" Marks the Spot

41 The Mare's Trick

42 Pair of Tongs

43 The Spinner

44 Back to Meditating

45 The Pin

46 Spoon-on-Spoon

47 Stretched Spoon-on-Spoon

48 Sliding Into Home

49 The Recliner

50 The Wrap Around

51 The Bucking Bronco

52 Will You Do Me?

53 Crouching Tiger, Hidden Passion

54 Let Us Pray

55 The Body Hug

56 Flexed Body Hug

57 Reclining Body Hug

58 Crying Out

59 Sweet Abandon

60 The Corkscrew

61 The Flexed Corkscrew

62 Inverted Headlock

63 The See-Saw A

64 The See-Saw B

65 The Backbend A

66 The Throne

67 See Spot Come

68 The Dutch Doggy

69 Taking Sides

70 The Back Scratcher

71 Enveloped in Love

72 Baby Elephant

73 Open Elephant

74 The Elephant

75 Sitting Body Wrap

76 Sitting Flexed Body Wrap

77 The Backbend B

78 The Pushover

79 The Cobra

80 The Pilot

81 The Stick Up

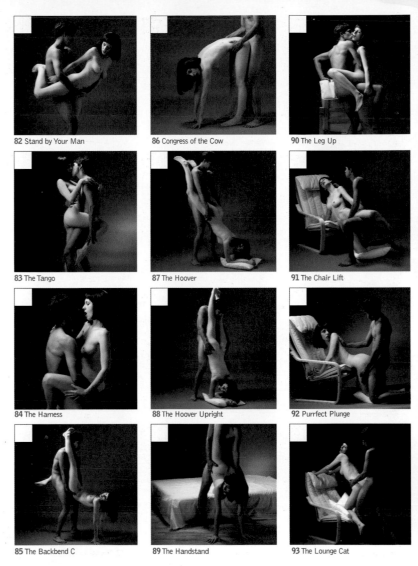

82 Stand by Your Man

83 The Tango

84 The Harness

85 The Backbend C

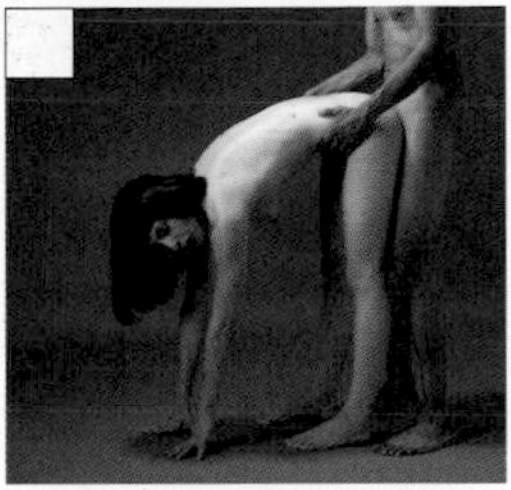

86 Congress of the Cow

87 The Hoover

88 The Hoover Upright

89 The Handstand

90 The Leg Up

91 The Chair Lift

92 Purrfect Plunge

93 The Lounge Cat

94 Fido's on His Feet

95 The Wheelbarrow

96 Lay-Z Girl

97 Tug of War

98 Come Sit on My Lap

99 In Reverse

100 My Knight, My Chair

101 Chair Twister

102 Backseat Driver

103 Prepare for Takeoff

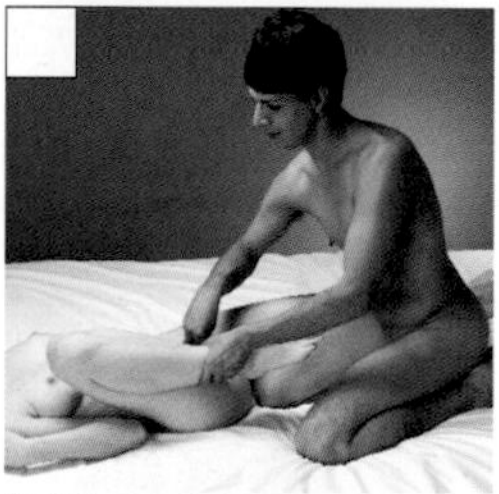

104 The Magic Lamp

105 Third Wish

106 Cat in the Cradle

107 Spank Her Thrice

108 The Double Grip

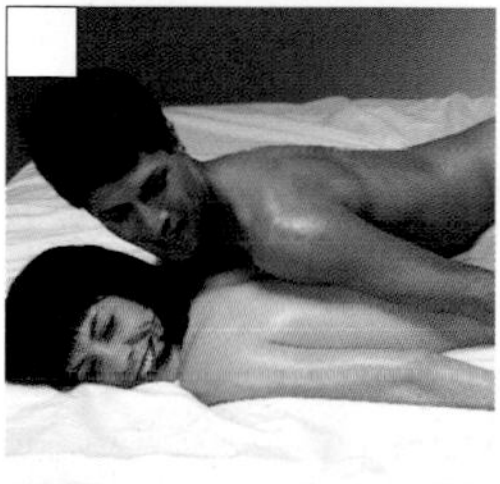

109 The Slippery Slope

110 Jigsaw

111 Put You on a Pedestal

112 Under the Hood

113 Pumping Petrol

114 Sweet Spot

115 Australian for Sex

116 Rising Sun

117 The Dip

118 The Bird Feeder

119 Chasing the Cat

120 Seat of Honor

121 Give and Take

122 Downtown Girl

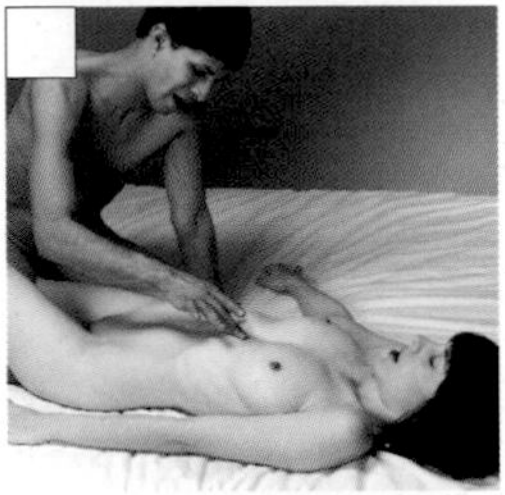
123 Slippery When Wet

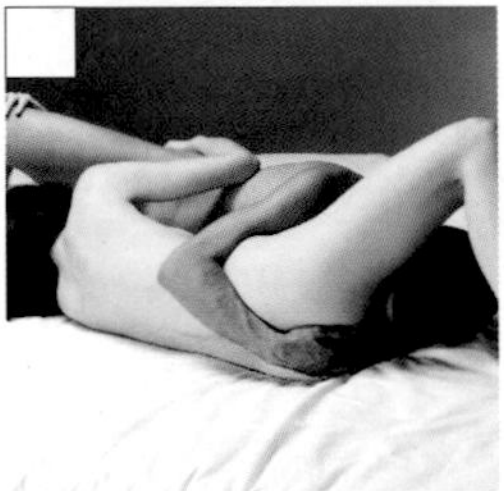
124 Always on Your Side

125 The Grateful Hostage

126 A Bridge to Pleasure

127 Tunnel of Love

128 Checking the Oil

129 Bumper Cars

130 Back in the Saddle

131 The Plow

132 My Door Is Always Open

133 The Nexus

134 Elephants on Parade

135 Table Saw

136 Queen of the World

137 Fantasy City

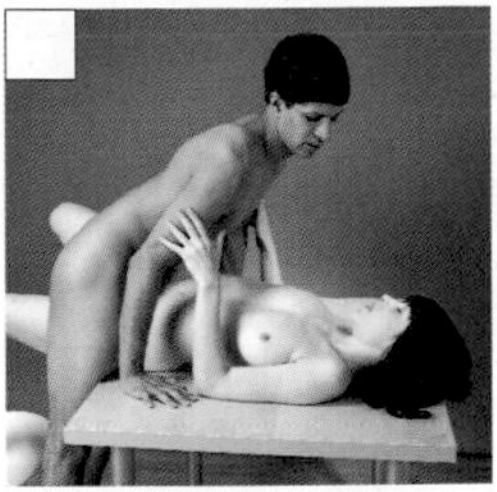

138 The Dinner Party

139 The Kissing Lotus

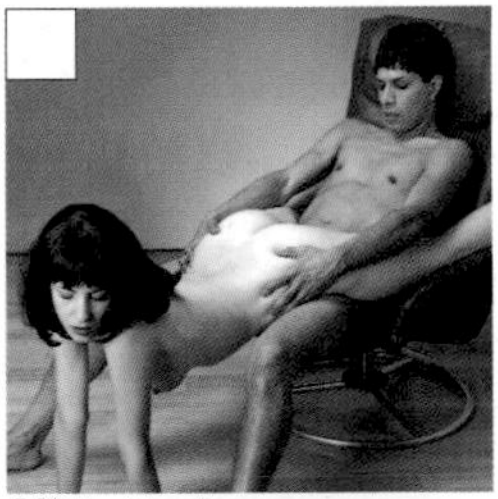

140 The Sheath

141 Members Only Entrance

142 Lean on Me

143 The Consolation

144 Lady Godiva

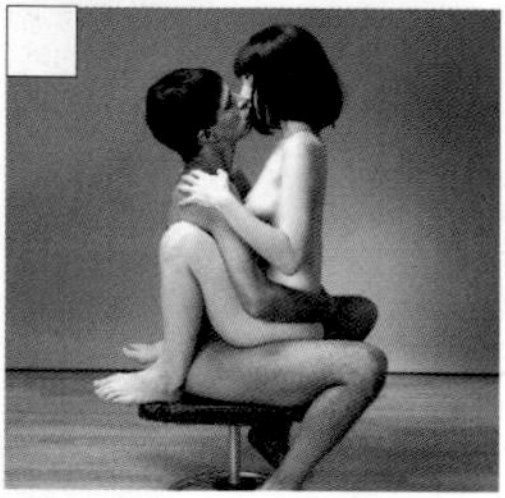
145 Bare Hug

146 Cupid's Bow

147 Tight Quarters

148 I've Found My Niche

149 The Long and Deep of It

150 Into Each, His Own

151 The Door Jam

152 Climbing the Walls

153 Synchronized Deep Diving

154 Long Night, Full Moon

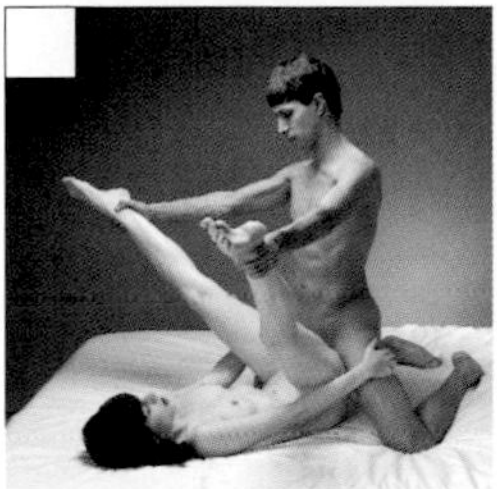

155 Spreading Some Joy

156 Deep Satisfaction

157 Surfing the Wave

158 Leapfrog

159 Blooming Lotus

160 Speaking in Tongues

161 The Nail-Gun

162 Praying Mantis

163 Lowered Inhibition

164 Meet Me in the Middle

165 Studying Geometry

166 Behind the Scenes

167 Hopping the Fence

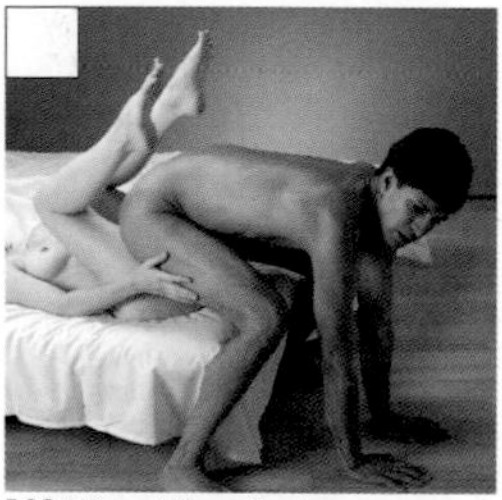

168 I Saved Your Seat

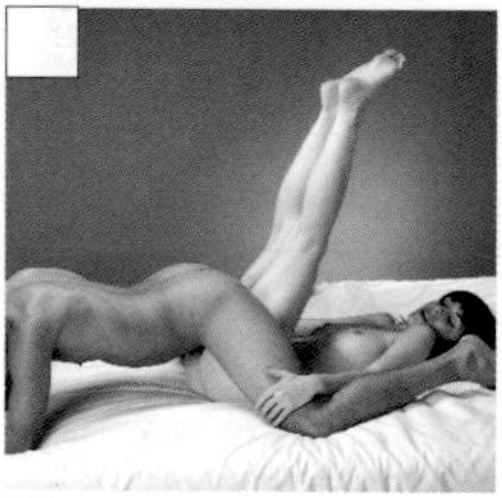

169 Upside Down You Turn Me

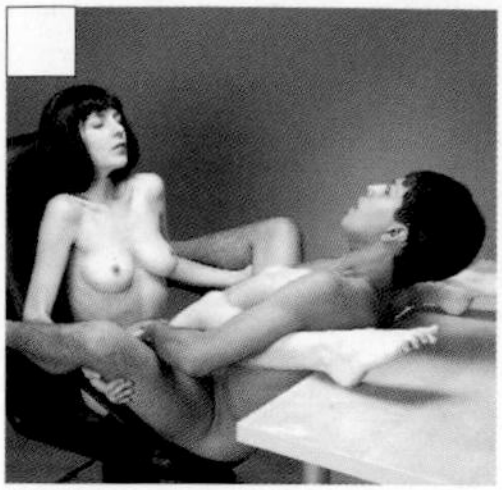

170 The Corporate Merger

171 The Motivator

172 Working Your Way Up

173 Out of the Box

174 Power Broker

175 Giving Her a Raise

176 Entry-Level Position

177 Loving Takeover

178 Climbing the Ladder

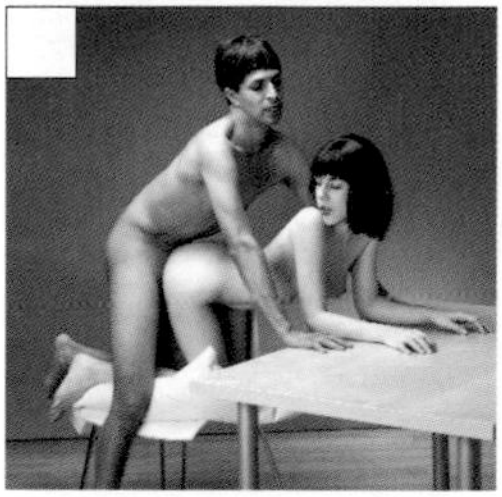

179 Behind on Work

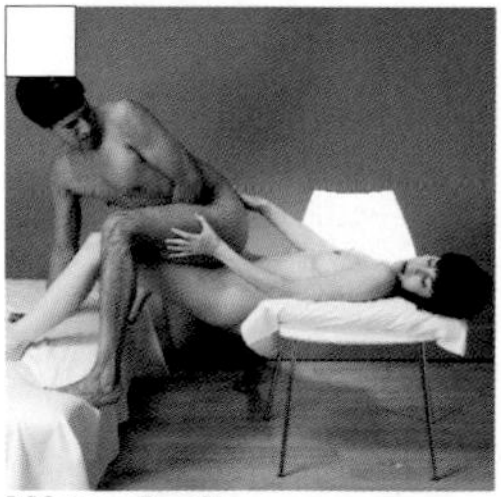

180 Flex Benefits

181 Double Shift

182 The Profit Share

183 Take a Letter Please

184 Sharing Your Assets

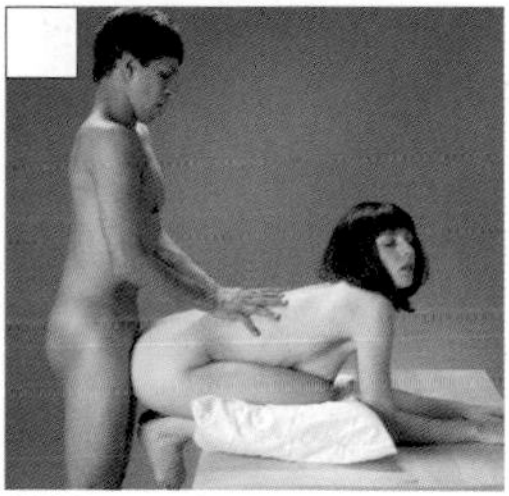

185 Squeeze Me In

186 The Ruthless Negotiator

187 Appealing to Your Target Market

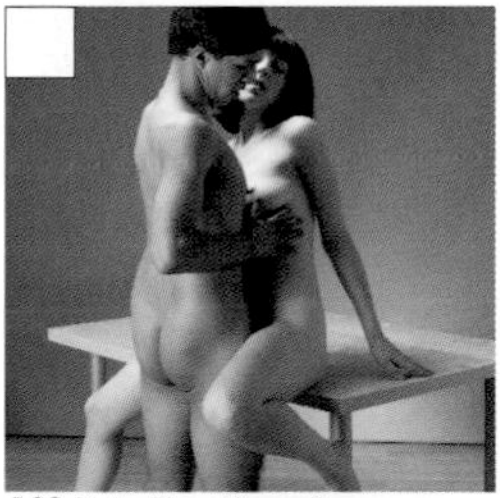

188 Better Than Phone Sex

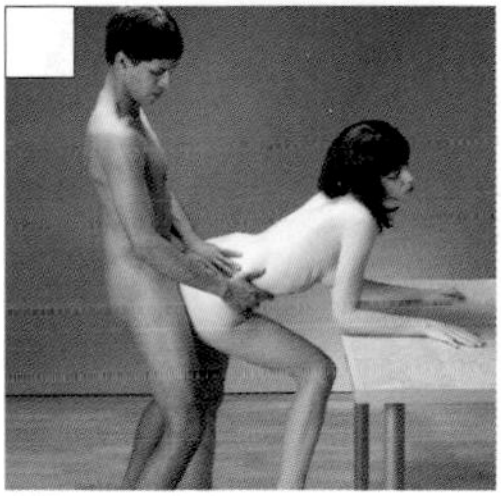

189 Tight Schedule

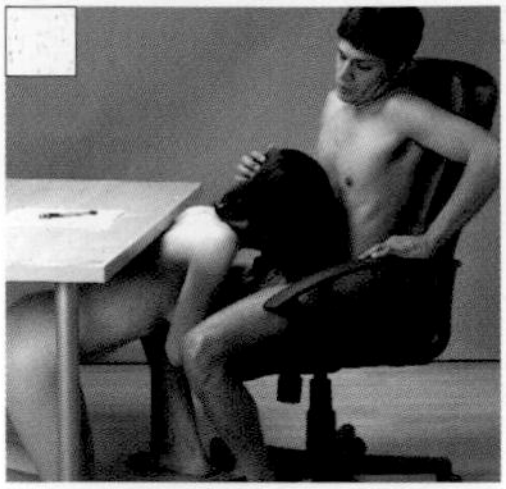

190 Getting the Memo

191 Rough Rider

192 Performance Art

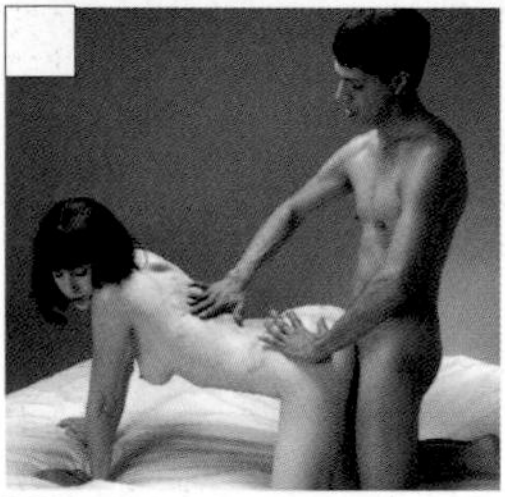

193 Smear Tactics

194 Prisoner of Love

195 Love Slave

196 Impaled Passion

197 Working Every Angle

198 Trapped Bumblebee

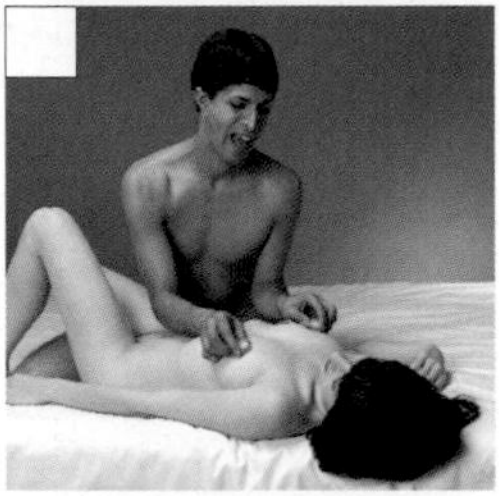

199 Fire and Ice

200 The Earthquake

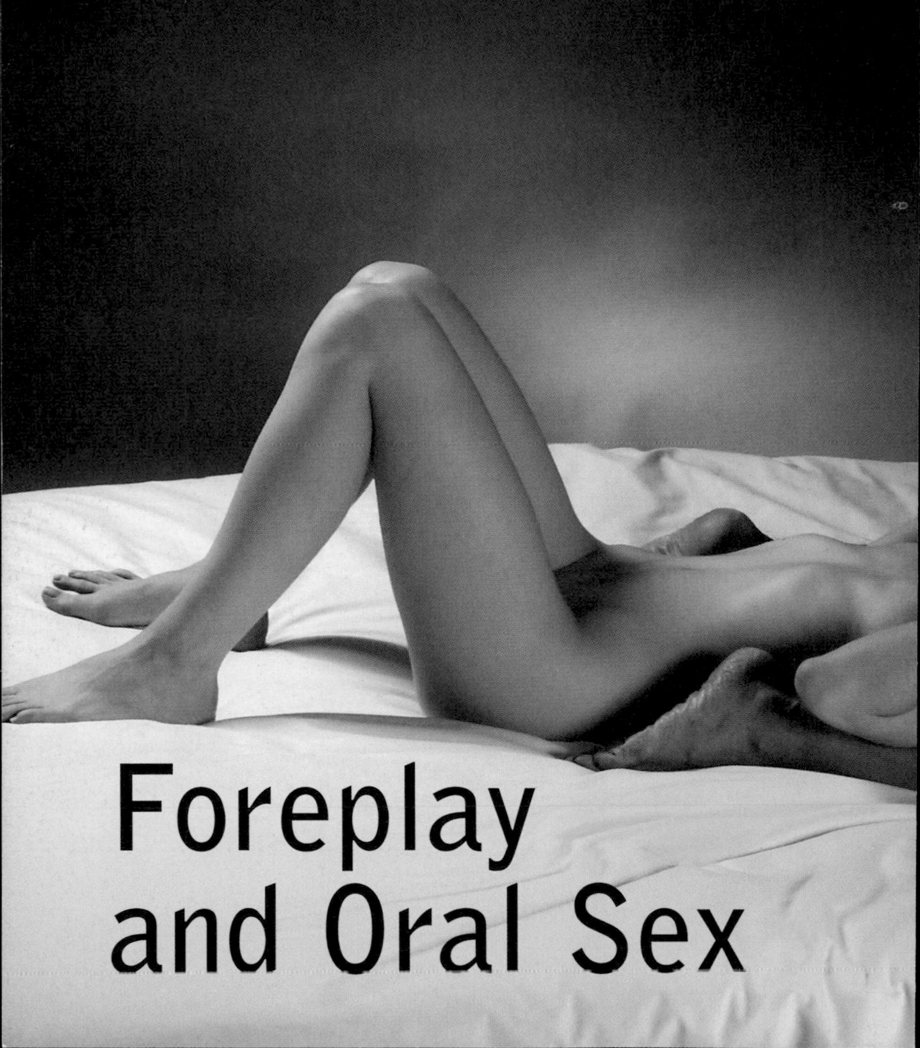

Foreplay and Oral Sex

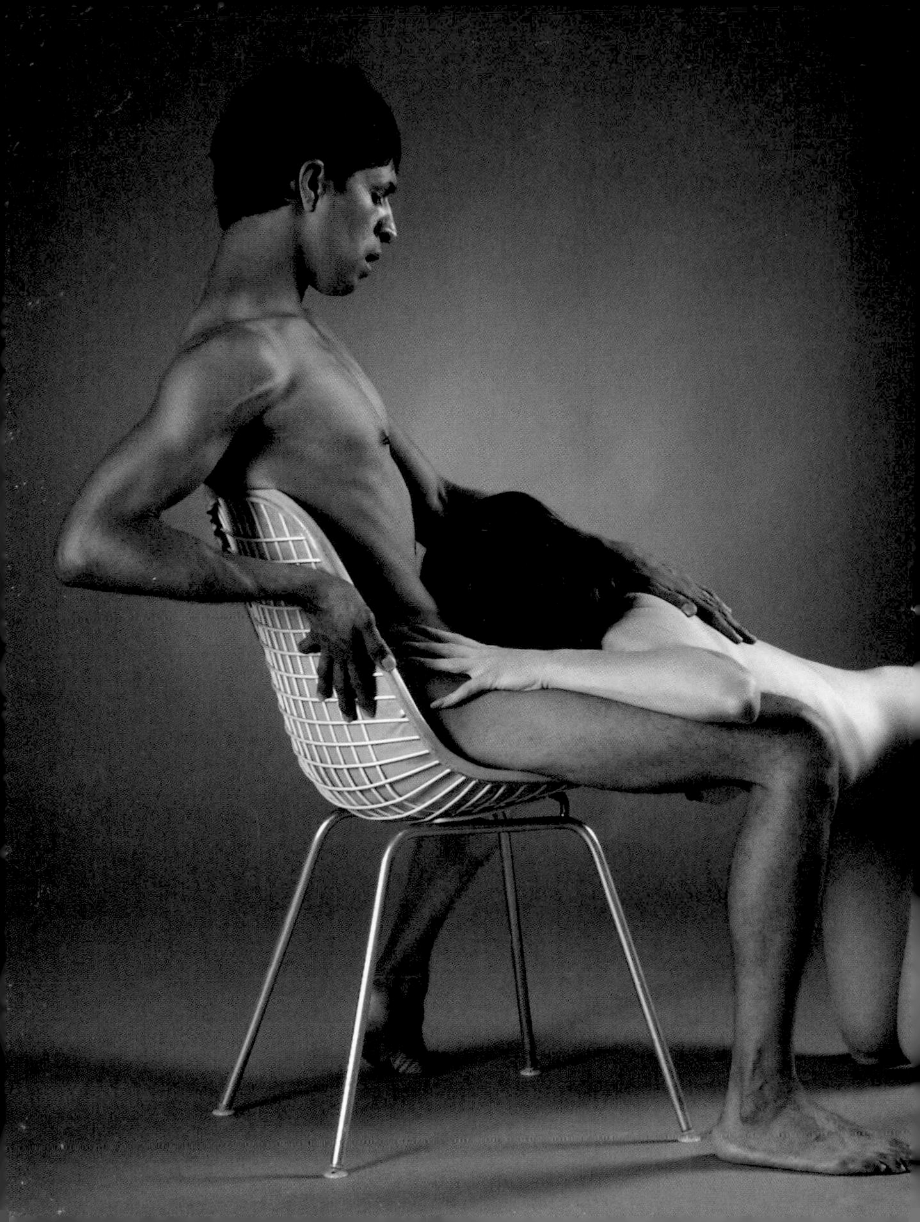

201

The Classic

Sitting down, the man is pleasured orally by the woman, who kneels before him. He is able to enjoy the view from this position of power. His hands are free to caress her head, but this position is focused on him.

202

Eating In

Allowing the woman full control, the man lies on the bed with his head over the edge. She sits spread above him and straddles his face as he explores her most delicate parts with his lips and tongue, bringing her to climax.

203

Stand and Deliver

He stands behind the chair, and asks, "Yes?" Wearing a blindfold, she kneels beside the chair and leans over it, clasping the side of the seat with both hands and elbows at her side. She replies, "Yes." He rests one hand on her back, holding her securely in place as he firmly slaps her buttocks before gently tickling her anus.

204

Nose to the Grindstone

Still blindfolded, she kneels on the floor and sits on her feet with her hands tied securely behind her back. Holding her shoulder, he bends his knees slightly and guides her head to lick and suck his testicles and penis.

205

Take It Sitting Down

The woman sits before the man and pleasures him with her mouth. More comfortable for the giver than the typical kneeling position, the man receiving fellatio here will appreciate his partner's added attention as he is penetrated anally.

206

The Happy Puppy

The woman lies on her back and the man kneels on top of her, doggie style. She is given a full view of him as she takes him into her mouth, leaving a hand free to massage his testicles or finger his anus.

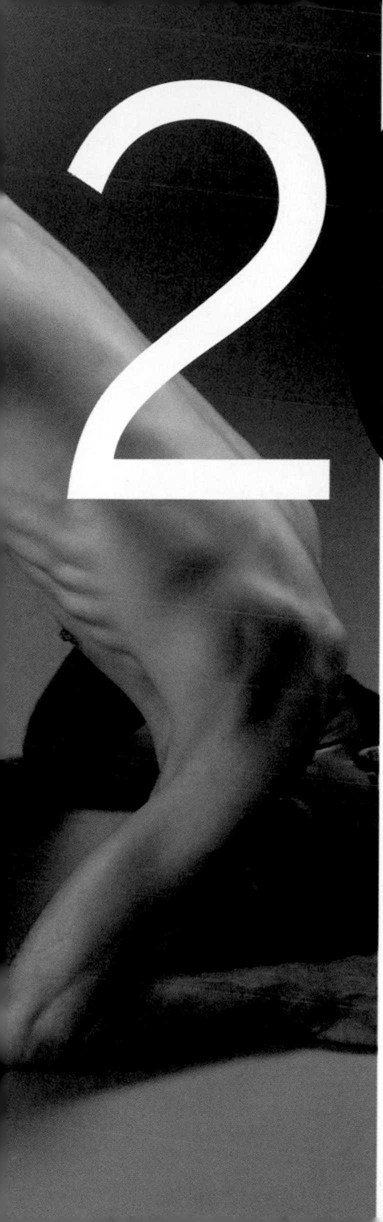

207

The Ben Dover

As the man bends over, he opens himself up for her tongue to stimulate his anus. She uses her free hands to touch his penis, giving him two pleasures for the price of one.

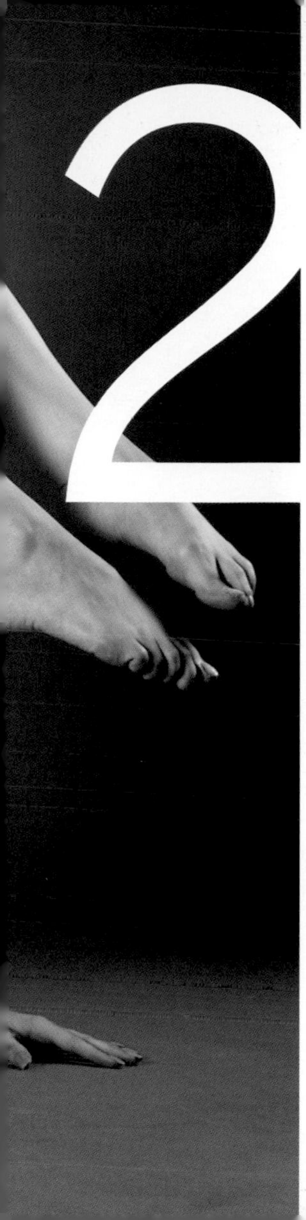

208

The Circle of Pleasure

The woman lies on the floor and is lifted by the man, who bends slightly over her to pleasure her with his tongue. She is able to return the favor by touching him with her two free hands.

209

Kiss My . . .

As the woman stands with her bottom slightly out, the man sits and pleasures her with his mouth. She can keep her hands on the back of his head, and control the depth of his tongue. From this position, the woman can fantasize that anyone, including her partner, is behind her, making her come.

210

The Elevator

She raises her legs and balances on her shoulders as he bends down to perform cunnilingus on her, supporting her back and stomach. This can easily be modified for multi-partner sex, but we'll leave that to your imagination.

211

The Landscape of Two Mountains

The man lies on his back with knees bent as the woman straddles his face, leaning her weight on his chest. He proceeds to provide oral sex while lifting her up with his hands on her behind, giving himself room to breathe.

212

The Curled 69

The man and woman perform oral sex on each other simultaneously, but curl into a tucked position to create a tighter, more intimate position as they cradle each other into orgasm.

213

Slap and Tickle

The man sits in a chair with the woman standing beside him. She stretches herself over his lap, supporting herself on her hands and the tips of her toes. He holds her by pressing the lower half of his arm to keep her firmly in place, while he spanks and strokes her buttocks, making her bottom red, tingly, and hot.

214

Oh, Adam, What an Apple

The man lies face up so that his head is at or near the edge of the bed; the woman straddles his face, keeping her feet on the floor and lowers her vagina to his mouth. He can use his hands to stimulate her clit and her anus.

215

Give Him a Hand

The reversal of the Slap and Tickle, the man extends himself over the lap of his partner and is spanked repeatedly, turning his bottom a pleasurable shade of apple red.

216

O Marks the Spot

He leans on the edge of the bed and straddles his partner, who is bent before him. He licks her anus and fingers her clitoris and nipples, stimulating several erogenous zones at once to create a powerful orgasm.

217

Mistress May I?

Blindfolded, the man crouches on the floor with his hands secured around him with his tie. The woman stands before him and, cupping her hands around his head, guides his mouth to her nether regions and instructs him to do precisely what she desires.

218

The Sack of Potatoes

As the man lifts the woman by her hip and turns her slightly, she stimulates his penis with one hand, while caressing his body with the other.

Taking It to Another Level

219

The Cradle

While in the missionary position, the man brings his legs up to cradle his partner, as he slowly kisses her breasts, creating a sensual and intimate moment for the two.

220

Hammocking

Squatting to form a chair, the man takes the woman onto his lap, rocking back and forth on the balls of his feet. The woman might want to take control and rock—letting their bodies fall where they may.

Salted or Unsalted?

The man spreads his legs horizontally and enters the woman, who opens her legs in the opposite direction. She leans back and grasps his leg for support as she orgasms in this delicious pretzel of pleasure.

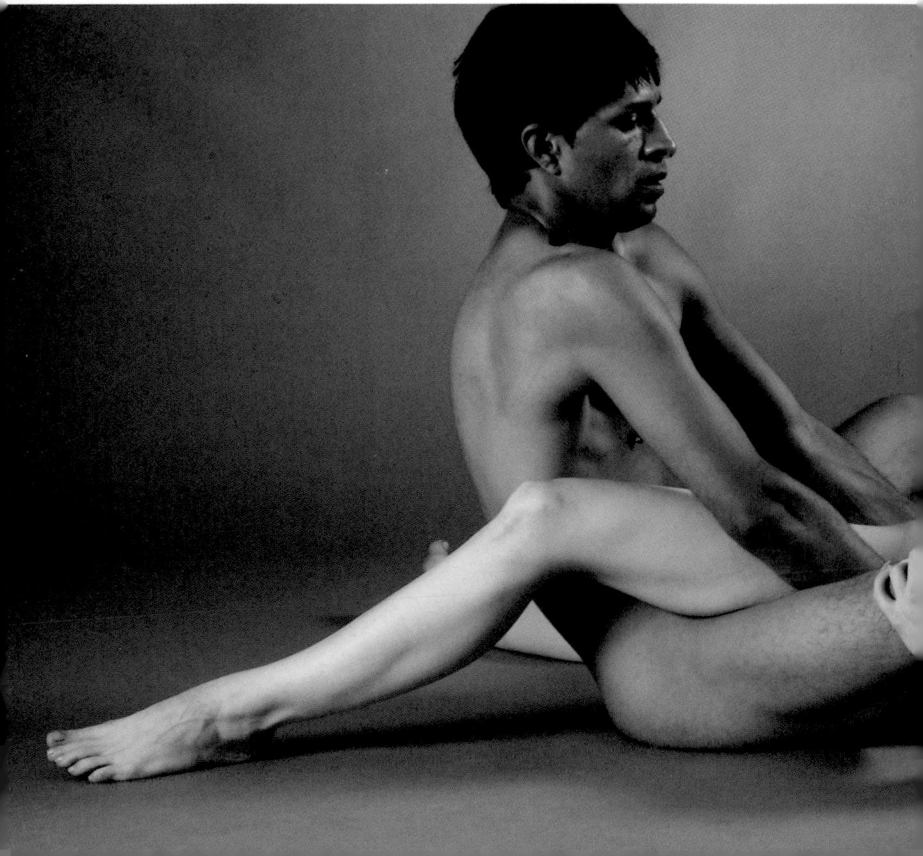

221

222

Learning to Walk

She lies on her back on the bed with her feet resting on the floor. He straddles her, facing away from her and enters her upside-down and hanging off the bed, using his arms for balance. She wraps her left leg around his back and to his right shoulder.

The Golden Eagle

She lies facedown on the bed with one leg perpendicular to the edge of the bed and the other hanging off. He stands beside the bed and straddles her hanging leg, entering her; she raises her hanging leg to go between his legs and rub against his testicles.

223

Crossing the River

The man enters the woman from behind, arching his back and allowing her to imagine her deepest fantasies. He supports her with his leg, and the couple creates a bridge to paradise.

224

The Carriage House

She gets down on all fours, allowing him to kneel down and enter her from below. He now leans back and watches as she slides back and forth.

225

226

Catch You on the Flip Side

He lies face up on the bed, and facing away from him, she straddles him, bending her knees behind her, leaning back on her hands and sliding down to mount him. He loosely grazes his hands around her hips, helping her to pace her strokes.

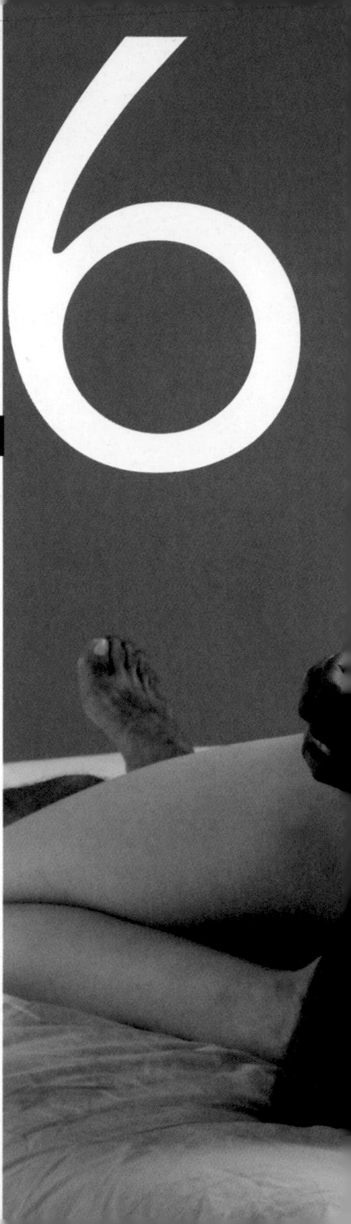

227

The Intertwined Links

Lying on their sides, head to toe, the couple merge their private parts. She may now kiss his feet or massage his testicles, while he should feel free to caress her buttocks and thighs.

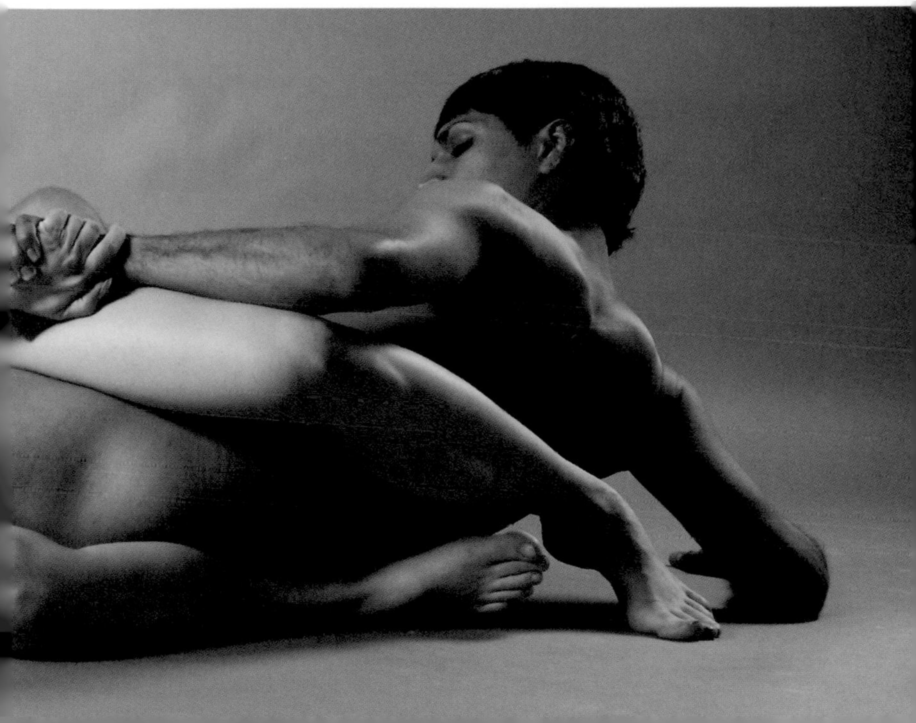

Chain Me Up

Lying on the floor with his legs in a V, the man enters the woman anally while she bridges over him, creating a chain link. This position requires effort, but is well worth it.

228

229

Shucking the Oyster

She rests her legs on the chair while keeping her weight on her arms as he enters her from behind and caresses her body with his hands.

230

Under Wraps

The man sits on a chair and wraps his legs around his partner's waist, as she supports him from below. She takes the lead and decides when and how deep to thrust.

231

The Kitchen Sink

She sits on his lap and balances herself with her hands on his thighs, squeezing as she orgasms. He is free to watch himself penetrate, as she spreads her legs over his shoulders.

232

Rock-a-Bye Baby

As he sits on a chair, she straddles him and leans forward as they clasp hands for support. If he is on a rocking chair, he might rock slowly, while he is afforded a beautiful view of her from behind, and she is rewarded with a feeling of flying.

233

The Curling Iron

The woman rests her torso on a rocking chair, and he enters her perpendicularly as she curls her legs around him. She can easily stimulate her clitoris, and he is free to stroke her whole body.

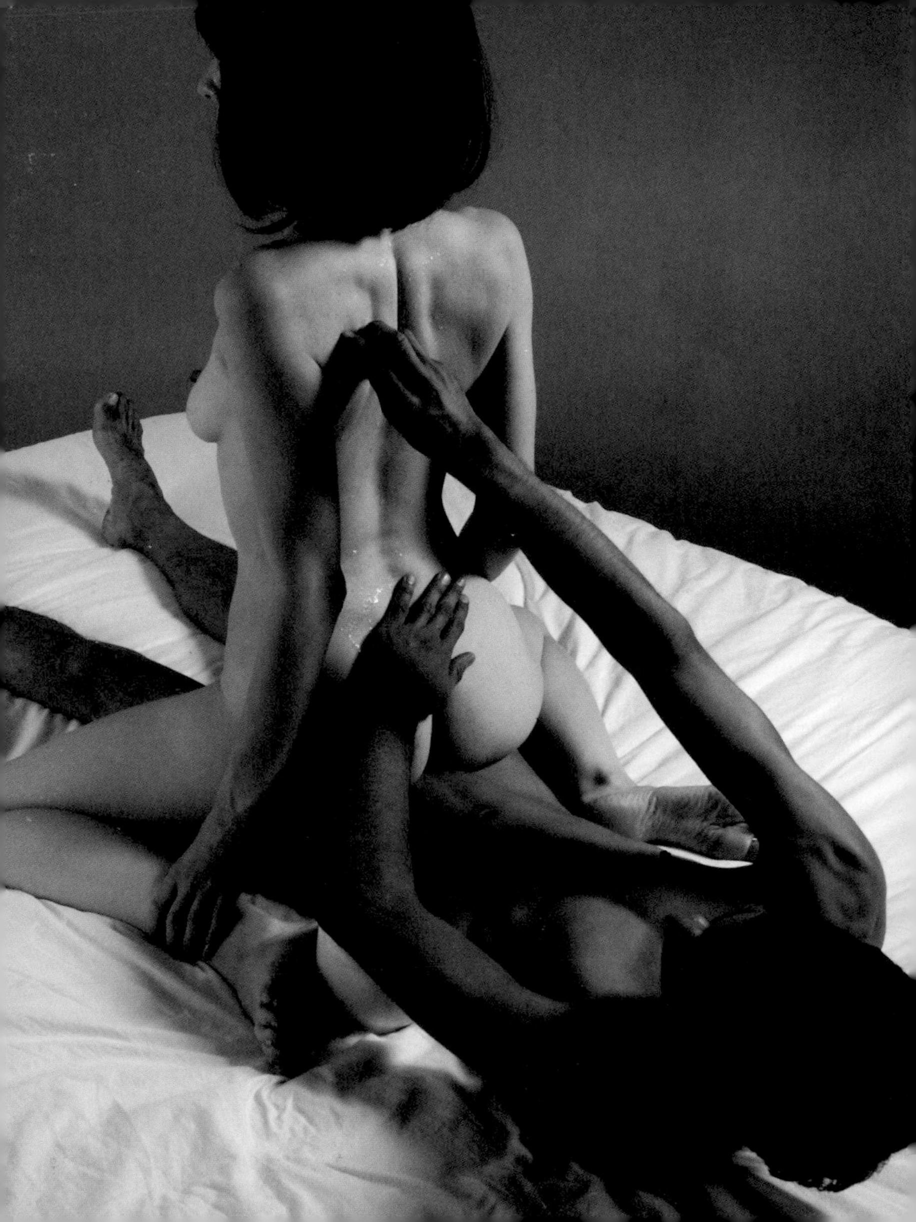

234

Like a Cat

He lies on the bed on his back, and she straddles him facing his feet, with her back arched. He rubs ice on her buttocks and back, cooling her kittenish heat.

235

On the Road

He bridges on his shoulders as she squats above him, grabbing one of his calves and pulling it forward, controlling his movement with as much precision as she would handle a standard shift automobile.

236

The Whoopie Cushion

Grasping the back of the chair, the man lifts himself up and balances on the seat on the balls of his feet, entering the woman, who stands before him, from behind. She holds the legs of the chair for extra support and balance.

237

Sailor's Knots

The man sits in a rocking chair as the woman leans down opposite him, raising her legs to rest behind his head. He rocks them back and forth while penetrating. This position can be reversed, and the woman is free to stimulate the man's prostate while taking the lead.

238

The Cancan Dancer

The woman raises one leg and rests it on the chair while she is penetrated from behind. Her hands are free to grab his thighs to pull him deeper into her, and his are free to caress her body.

239

The Venus Flytrap

The man lies back on an ottoman, lifting his bent legs, and takes the woman onto himself as she leans back into him. She can grasp onto his legs and caress his feet to increase his sensations.

240

The Homestretch

Resting his head on the chair, the man supports himself with his hands, and enters the woman, who holds her legs back and open as far as they'll go while lying on the ottoman. This stretch is a good preparation for the Three-Chair Double Squat.

241

The Three-Chair Double Squat

The woman squats between the man's legs, which he has spread open and supported by a chair each, as he leans back on the ottoman, supporting himself with his hands.

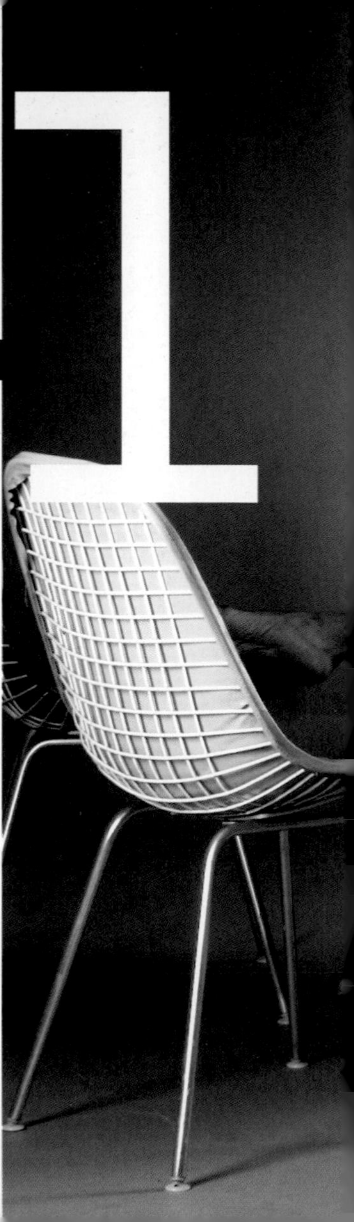

242

Doing Cartwheels

The man lies on his back and lifts his legs in a split. The woman then sits between his legs, allowing him to enter her. From this position, she is able to control every movement.

243

The Headstand of Pleasure

As the woman lies on the floor, the man lifts her so that she is parallel to him, supporting herself with her shoulders. They grasp behind each other's knees, an erogenous zone, and support each other this way.

244

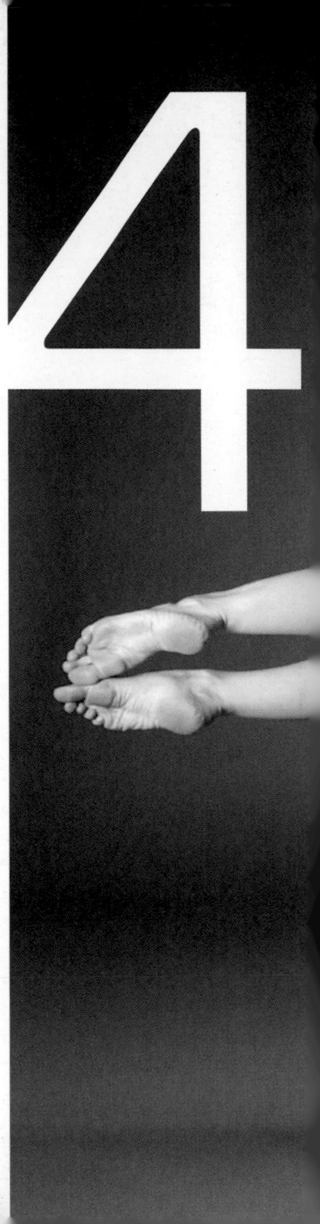

Pole Vaulting

The man lifts the woman sideways and enters her as she supports herself with her arms. He grasps her by the thighs and behind, so as to make her feel secure as well as pleasured.

Springing

As he crouches and lifts her legs and torso, she balances herself with her hand behind her head. With her free hand, she can touch herself, providing herself some pleasure and him a show, as he penetrates.

245

246

The Plow and Hoe

As the man lifts her legs around him, the woman supports herself with her two arms, bridging back in ecstasy. Here he controls the pressure and timing of the thrust as she balances back and enjoys.

247

Roll Your Rs

The woman balances on her hands as she leans against the man, putting her feet on his shoulders. He grabs her behind, supporting her while providing a pleasurable massage to her bottom, as she roars with rapture.

That's a Wrap

Curled up on the floor, the man enters the woman wrapped up in passion and cradling each other in an intimate and trusting position. The man is free to stimulate the woman's anus orally.

248

Mountain's Majesty

Facing opposite each other, the man penetrates the woman from behind and both raise their legs and bottoms to create a mountain of bliss.

249

250

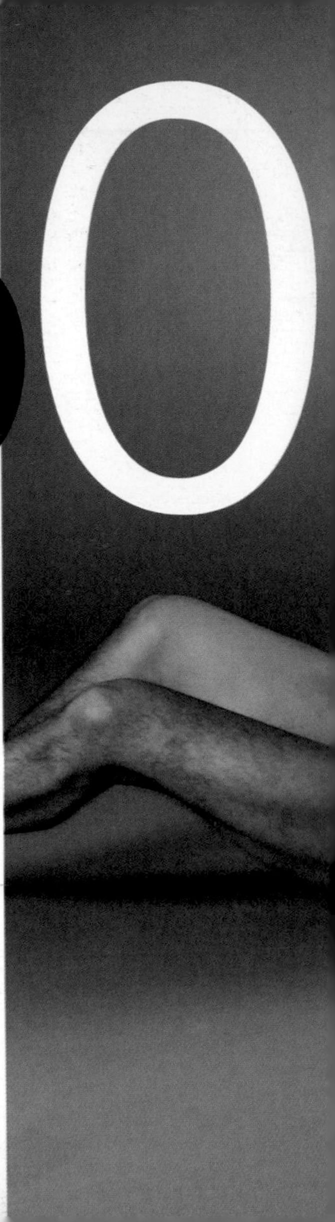

Crisscross Apple Sauce

He lies on the floor, legs crossed, and she sits on top of him, crossing her legs and stroking his face. The pressure that comes from her crossed legs is sure to give him intense and tight pleasure.

251

Welcome Home

The man kneels and the woman crouches as she hugs him and he enters her. A highly intimate position, both partners' hands are free to explore various erogenous zones.

252

Ice Hot

The woman bends in front of the man, who enters her from behind, controlling the rhythm of the act. At just the right moment, he places an ice cube to roam down her back, cooling her heated body.

253

What's for Dessert?

The woman lies on her back and takes the man, who sits between her legs. He holds her torso to maintain a steady thrusting rhythm, while licking chocolate paint from her nipples.

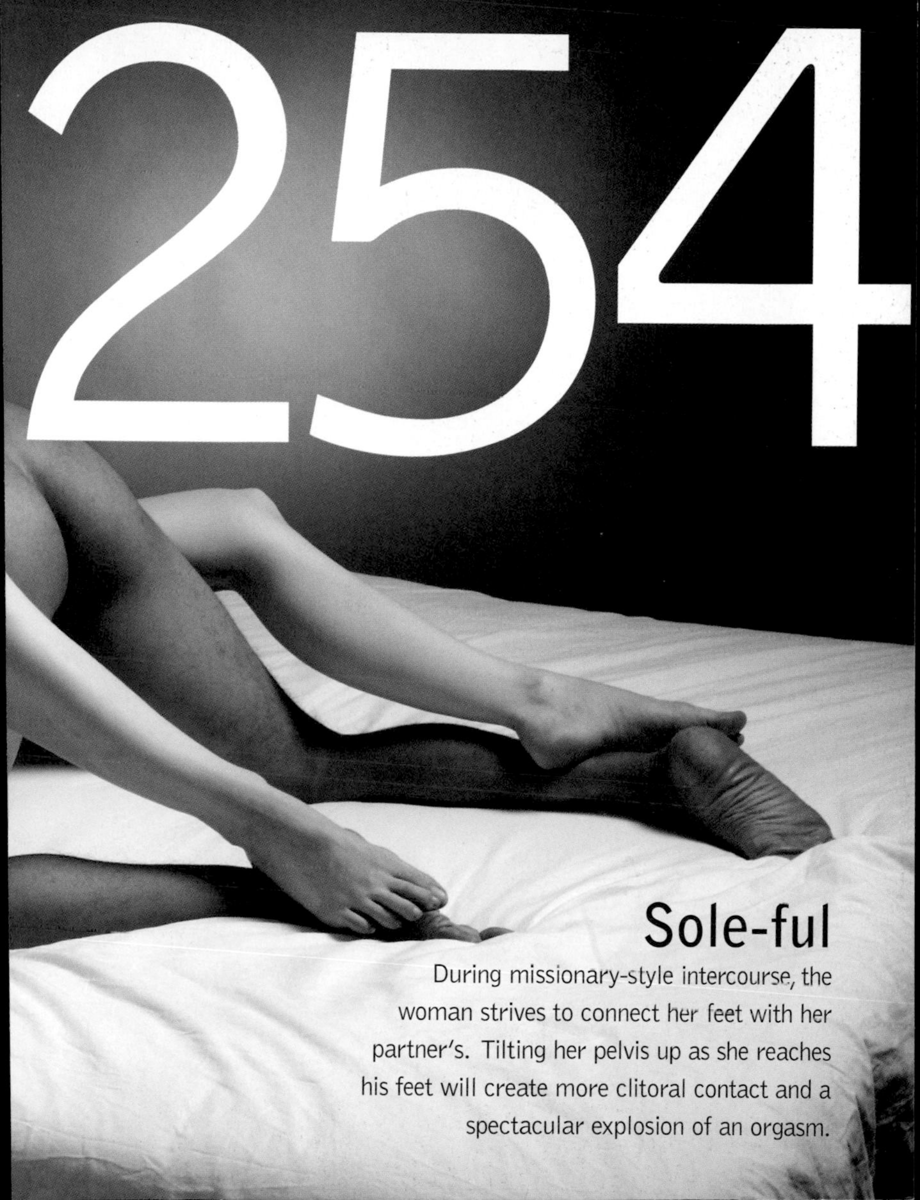

254

Sole-ful

During missionary-style intercourse, the woman strives to connect her feet with her partner's. Tilting her pelvis up as she reaches his feet will create more clitoral contact and a spectacular explosion of an orgasm.

255

Stiletto High-Rise

Wearing stilettos, she faces the wall, bracing her hands against it. With her added height, he can easily enter her from behind while fingering her anus.

256

See You Later

The woman lies on her back and raises her legs as the man sits facing the same direction and enters her. This leaves him open to fantasies, and renders her capable of scratching or rubbing his back.

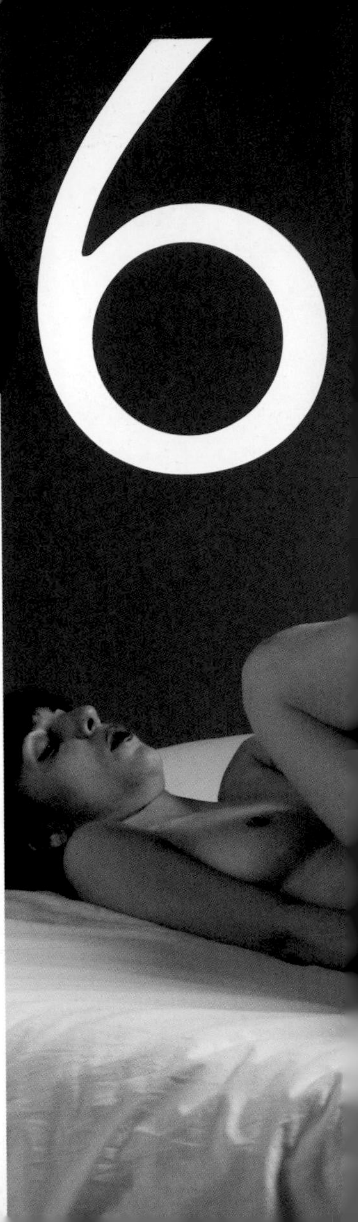

257

The Great Plains

The man enters the woman facing opposite her as her leg is bent to provide ample space for him. He is free to stimulate her feet and enter deeper than ever before, while she can anally stimulate him.

258

For Your Thighs Only

She bonds herself onto his penis and faces sideways and forward so that her clitoris rubs against his raised thigh, creating sizzling friction and an exciting climax.

259

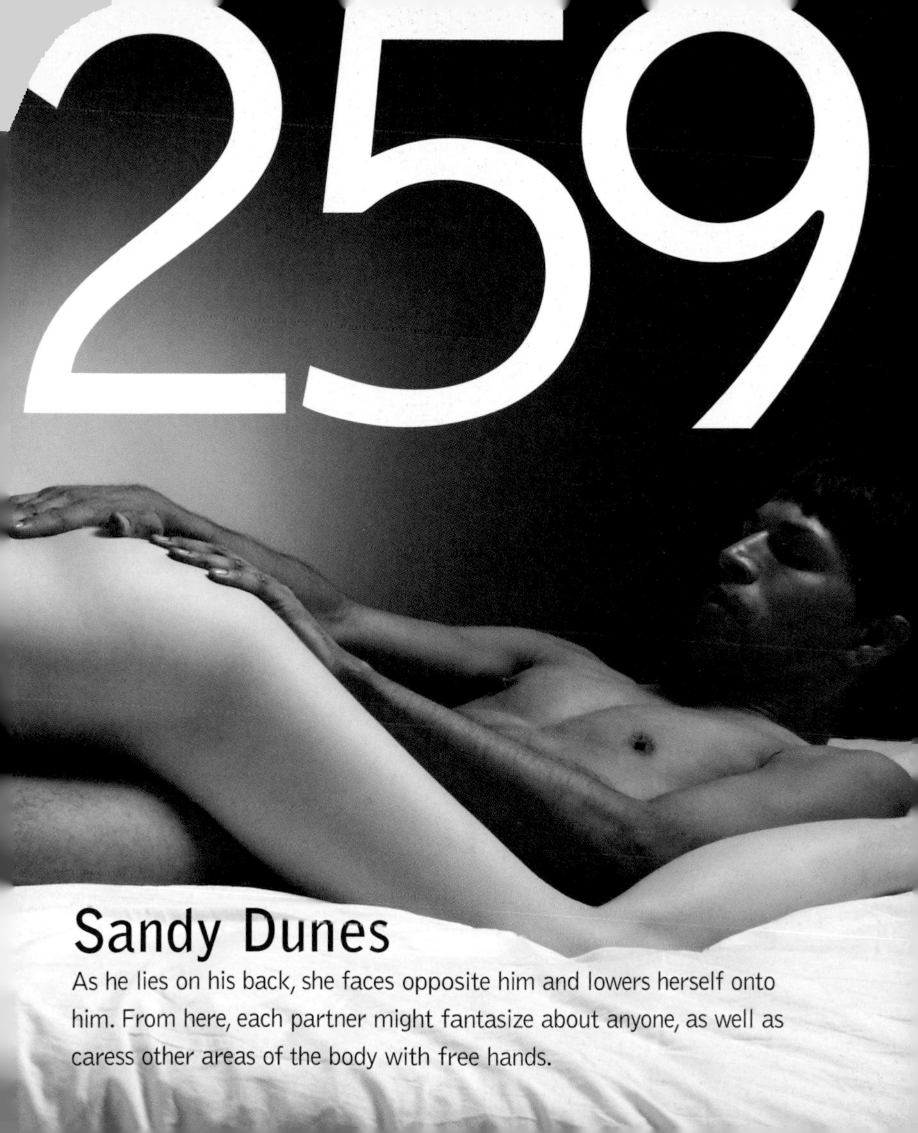

Sandy Dunes

As he lies on his back, she faces opposite him and lowers herself onto him. From here, each partner might fantasize about anyone, as well as caress other areas of the body with free hands.

260

Sail Away

She lies on her stomach, and he enters her from behind, lifting her leg to meet his back, allowing for deeper penetration and sending them on a voyage of titanic pleasure.

261

The T-Bone

The kneeling man lifts the woman's hips as she lies on the bed in front of him. He enters her from behind, using his free hand to stimulate her clitoris, creating a tender, juicy orgasm, cooked to perfection.

262

Rolling Hills

The man sits in the center of the bed, leaning back on a large cushion with his legs slightly open and his knees bent. The woman lies in the man's lap with her knees falling over his shoulders and her hands gripping his upper arms. He enters her, clasping her waist and rocking their bodies back and forth.

Ready, Set, Go!

The woman crouches on all fours before the man who is seated on the ottoman. He penetrates from behind, leaning back to give her the full length of himself.

263

The Black Spider

He lies on his back near the edge of the bed and swings his open legs up in the air. Facing away from him, she crouches on her hands and knees on the bed and leans back until their butts are touching. Then she pushes her elbows off the bed until her arms are fully extended and hangs one leg down off the side of the bed. He positions his penis to enter her and then fingers her clit.

264

265

The Intimate Hip Grasp

Kneeling on a kitchen chair, the couple can be adventurous in their setting, but maintain an intimacy as he enters her from behind and holds her hips close to his. He is also free to fondle her breasts and stimulate her clitoris.

266

Fighter Planes

She lies faceup and parallel to the edge of the bed, with her arms by her sides; he lifts her legs up until they are at a 45-degree angle to her body; then he enters her so that he is perpendicular to her body, supporting his weight with one foot and one arm and raising the others as if flying.

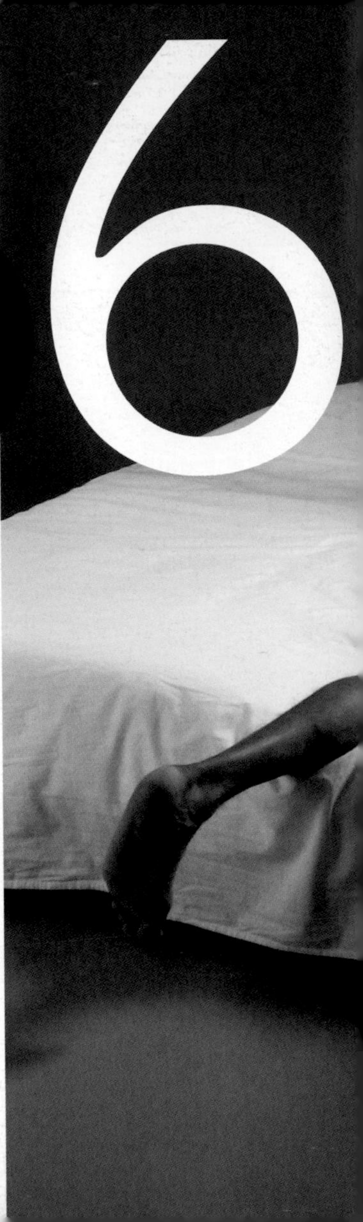

267

Riding into the Sunset

The man lies on his back on the bed and pushes his bottom up off the bed (like an old-fashioned bicycle exercise) and lifts his legs, bringing his knees toward his chest. She straddles his body and slides down onto his erect penis. She then bends and straightens her knees, controlling the thrusts.

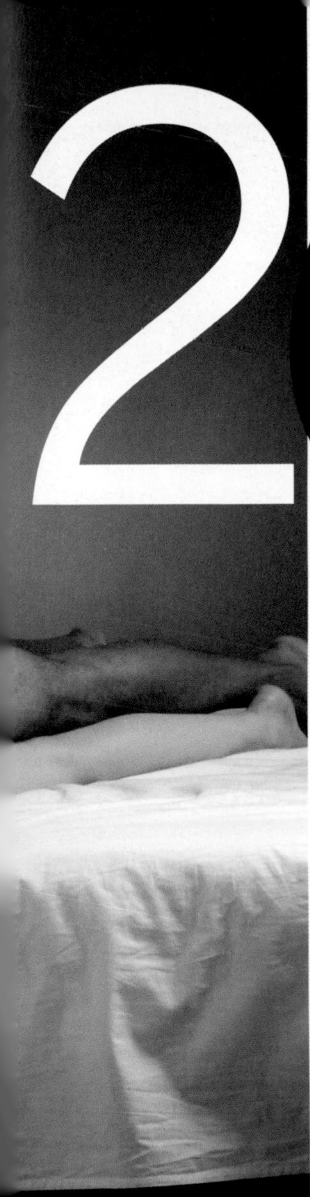

268

The Alligator

She lies on bed with her top half hanging off facing the floor, using her hands on the floor to support her. He enters her anally and holds his upper half off of her so that their top halves are at a 90-degree angle.

Linking Logs

He lies on his side on the bed with his legs hanging off; she straddles his legs with her top half hanging off the bed and her arms out for support.

269

The Most Beautiful Flower

He sits on the bed slightly away from edge, and she sits on him and slides herself onto his penis. She wraps legs around his bottom, and he holds her by the forearms as she relaxes and reclines almost to the floor, and he pulls her toward him and slowly lets her fall away.

270

271

The Contortionist

She starts on all fours and proceeds to rest on her shoulder and head. The man squats above her, penetrating her well-lubed anus and using her as a seat in this unusual and unusually pleasing position.

The Cricket

He lies on his back on the bed with knees bent and to the side; she lies on top of him with her back to him, and he holds her legs spread open and penetrates from behind. He is able to squeeze her legs closed for a tighter fit.

272

273

Flambé

He lies on his back on the bed and holds his left leg up and out in contact with her right hip; she kneels in between his legs and rides him while both garnish each other with chocolate body paint.

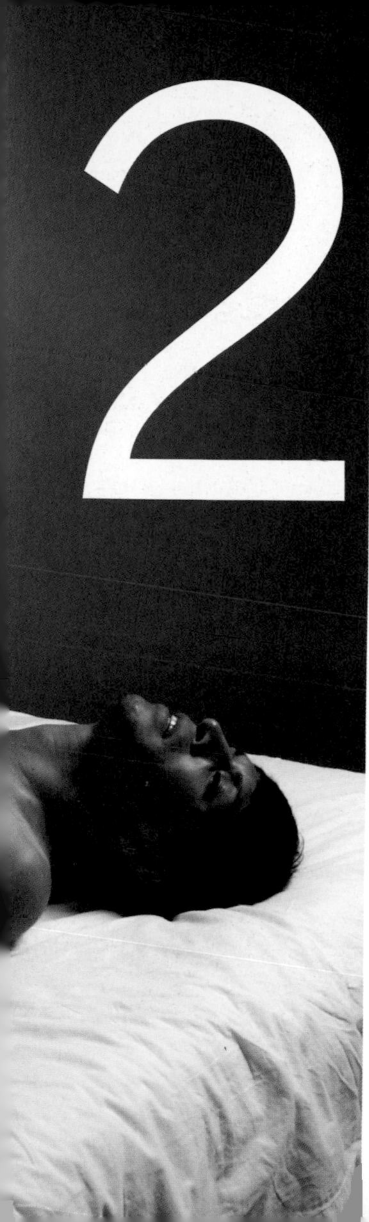

274

Hottest Snow

The man lies on his back on the bed; the woman straddles and sits on his penis, her legs bent under her. They massage each other with ice cubes to quench their fiery passion for just a moment.

275

Vroom, Vroom

As his lover lies facedown on the bed, the man should penetrate her while standing behind her, and lift her by the hips as she grasps onto his arms for support as she orgasms in the air.

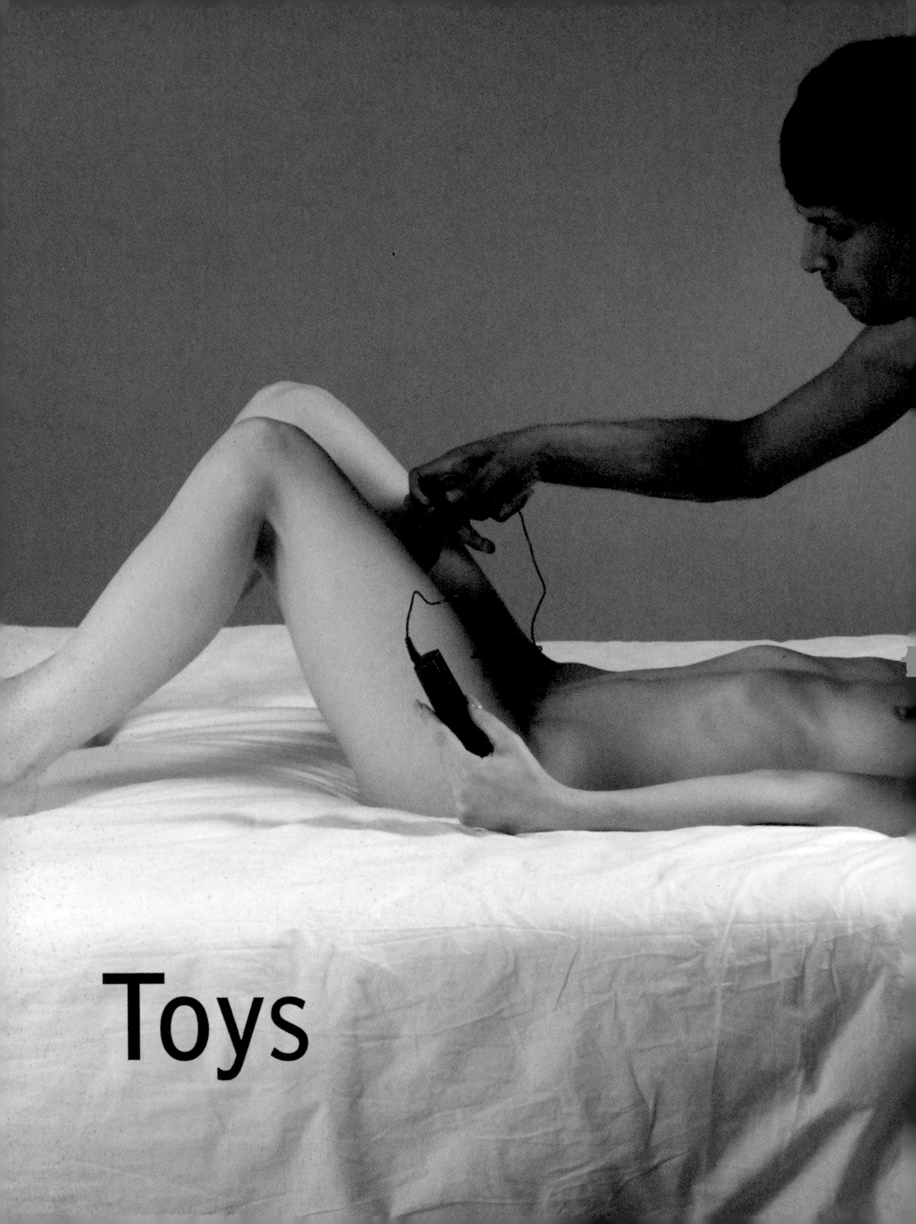

Toys

276

From Both Sides Now

Lying on the edge of the bed, the man takes the woman on top of him and uses a toy to anally penetrate her as he enters her vaginally.

277

Good Vibrations

She sits on edge of bed with a dildo; he bends forward, resting his hands on his knees. She penetrates with the dildo and perhaps stimulates his penis manually.

278

Hugging the Pole

The woman lies on her right side on the bed and pulls one leg up into the air (like a half-split); man kneels in front of her and rubs his penis against her raised leg, and she rests her leg on his shoulder; he inserts a dildo into her and strokes both.

279

Missile Launcher

A quick move from Fighter Planes (#266), the woman uses her left hand to insert an anal plug, allowing him to feel weightless and grounded at the same moment.

280

The Impaled Seesaw

The man leans back on his knees and enters his lover anally, as she inserts her string of pearls and stimulates her clitoris. He supports himself on his fists and pulls the toy out slowly as they climax.

281

Pulling the Plug

A quick movement from Under Wraps (#230), here the man flips the woman onto her stomach, and uses a toy to doubly penetrate her, adding to the sensual experience for both of them.

282

Watch Out Behind You

Resting one lifted leg on the chair, the woman opens herself up for deep penetration with a toy. The man is free to move all around her, creating immense pleasure without having to remain stationary.

283

Acrobatics

The woman sits on a chair with the man lying below her. He brings her to orgasm using toys and his fingers, and she is free to watch from above. Her hands are loose to support her, or assist him by stimulating herself.

284

The Gladiator's Torch

Moving from The Circle of Pleasure (#208), the man enters the woman with a toy, leaving his mouth free to kiss up and down her legs, as he continues supporting her torso.

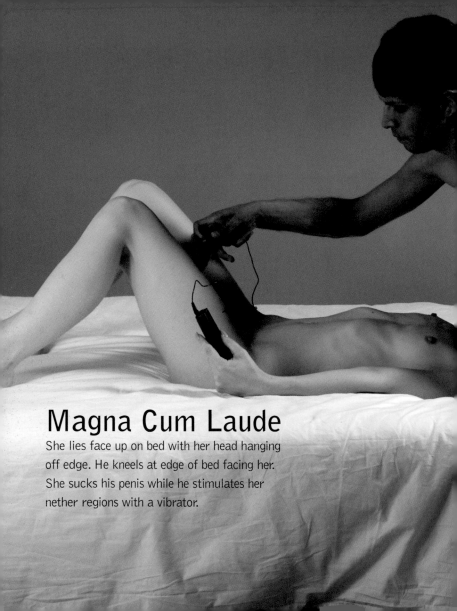

Magna Cum Laude

She lies face up on bed with her head hanging off edge. He kneels at edge of bed facing her. She sucks his penis while he stimulates her nether regions with a vibrator.

285

Swing Time!

286

The Shrieking Monkey

Practically weightless, the woman goes bananas as she swings freely back and forth onto her lover's tongue. He can alternate between manual and oral stimulation until she is shrieking with orgasm.

287

Sweet Chariot

The man stands while the woman crouches in the swing in front of him. This allows for deep penetration and a combination of bouncing and thrusting, all of which the man can enjoy without the overexertion related to lifting his partner.

288

Get Sprung

The woman sticks out her gorgeous behind, and is anally or vaginally penetrated from behind while the man stands, able to grip any part of her or the swing itself. As in Sweet Chariot (#287), each can fully enjoy bouncing and thrusting without worry of strain.

289

The Rocking Cradle

As the man sits in the swing, the woman lowers herself onto him, feeling every long inch of him in all new places as each leans back and rock gently, suspended and weightless.

290

Dinner for Two

With no worries of smothering the bottom partner, the couple engages in mutually beneficial oral sex. They bring each other to climax while swaying gently, enjoying the feel of air all over their bodies.

273 Flambé

274 Hottest Snow

275 Vroom, Vroom

276 From Both Sides Now

277 Good Vibrations

278 Hugging the Pole

279 Missle Launcher

280 The Impaled Seesaw

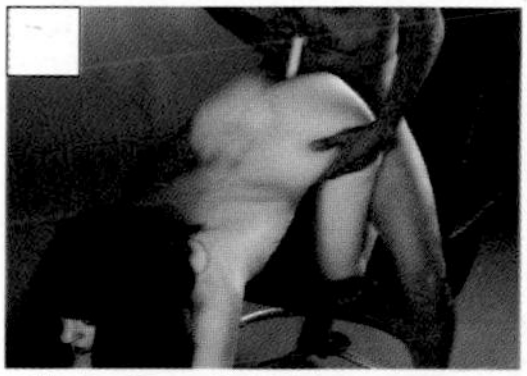
281 Pulling the Plug

282 Watch Out Behind You

283 Acrobatics

284 The Gladiator's Torch

285 Magna Cum Laude

286 The Shrieking Monkey

287 Sweet Chariot

288 Get Sprung

289 The Rocking Cradle

290 Dinner for Two

291 Dinner for One

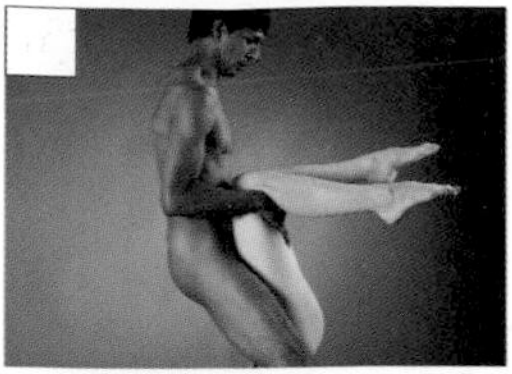
243 The Headstand of Pleasure

244 Pole Vaulting

245 Springing

246 The Plow and Hoe

247 Roll Your Rs

248 That's a Wrap

249 Mountain's Majesty

250 Crisscross Apple Sauce

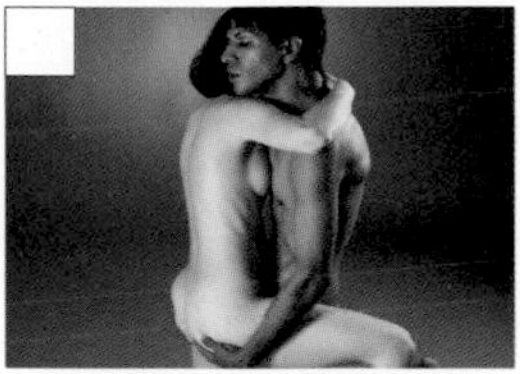
251 Welcome Home

252 Ice Hot

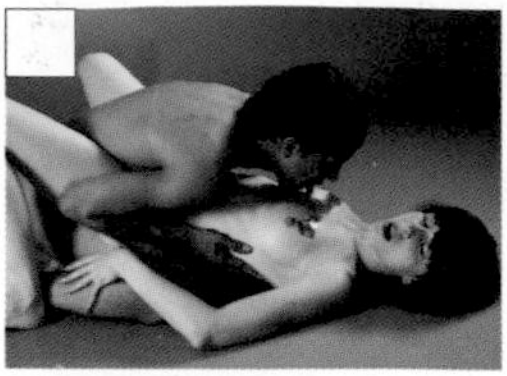
253 What's for Dessert?

254 Sole-ful

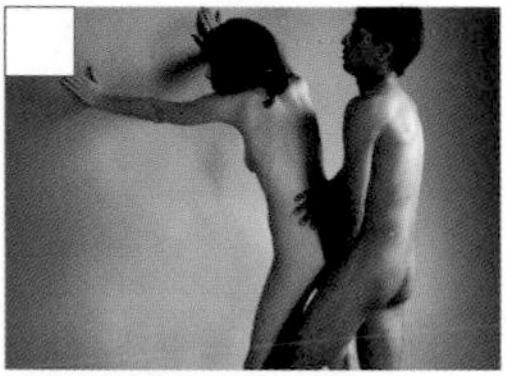
255 Stiletto High-Rise

256 See You Later

257 The Great Plains

258 For Your Thighs Only

259 Sandy Dunes

260 Sail Away

261 The T-Bone

262 Rolling Hills

263 Ready, Set, Go!

264 The Black Spider

265 The Intimate Hip Grasp

266 Fighter Planes

267 Riding into the Sunset

268 The Alligator

269 Linking Logs

270 The Most Beautiful Flower

271 The Contortionist

272 The Cricket

Checklist

This handy checklist is useful in many ways. Not only does it give you a thumbnail visual of each position for quick reference, but it also allows you to keep track of the positions as you enjoy them. Or, be creative and make icons for your favorite positions as well as those that will take some yoga classes to master!

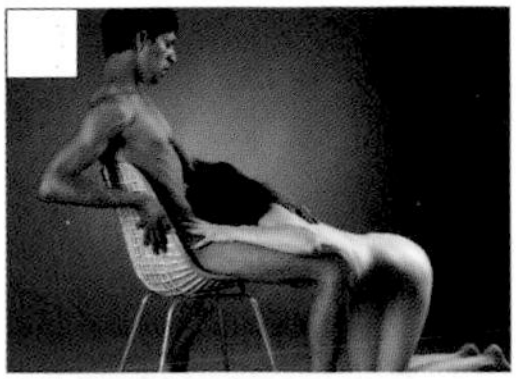

201 The Classic

202 Eating In

203 Stand and Deliver

204 Nose to the Grindstone

205 Take It Sitting Down

206 The Happy Puppy

207 The Ben Dover

208 The Circle of Pleasure

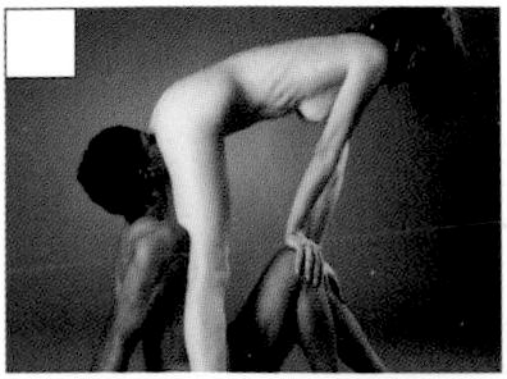

209 Kiss My . . .

210 The Elevator

211 The Landscape of Two Mountains

212 The Curled 69

291

Dinner for One

The woman arches her back in comfortable ecstasy, using her arms to control her pleasure level. The man crouches with his partner's feet planted on the floor or her legs draped over his shoulders, enjoying his meal.

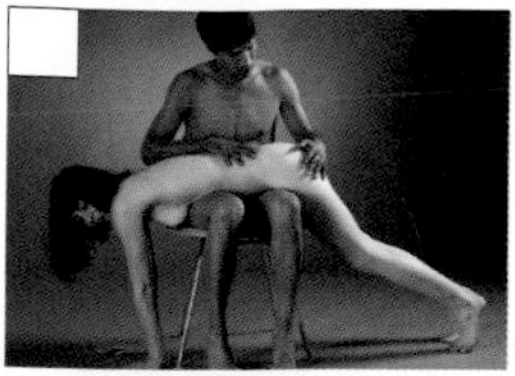
213 Slap and Tickle

214 Oh, Adam, What an Apple

215 Give Him a Hand

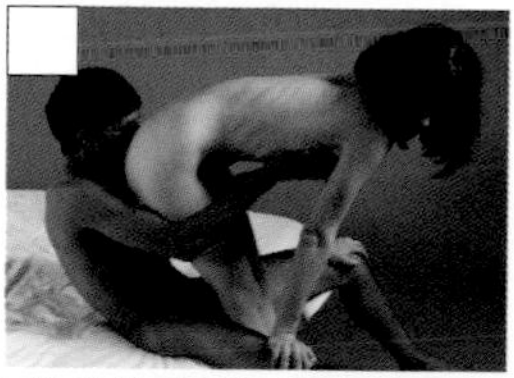
216 O Marks the Spot

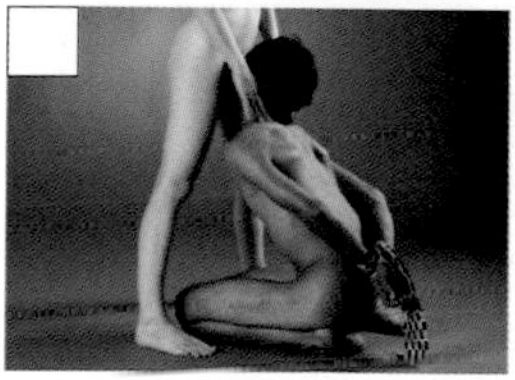
217 Mistress May I?

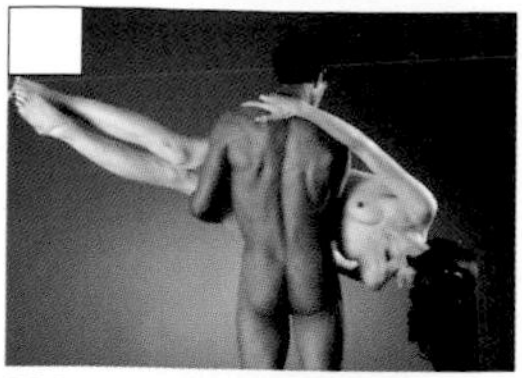
218 The Sack of Potatoes

219 The Cradle

220 Hammocking

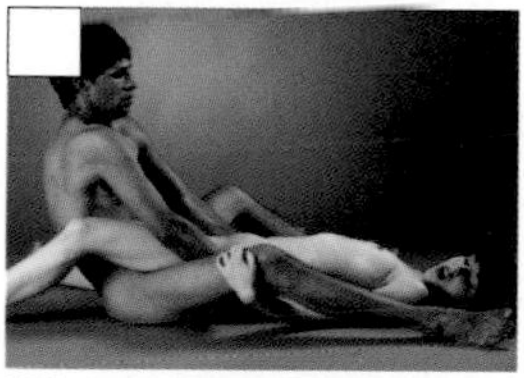
221 Salted or Unsalted?

222 Learning to Walk

223 The Golden Eagle

224 Crossing the River

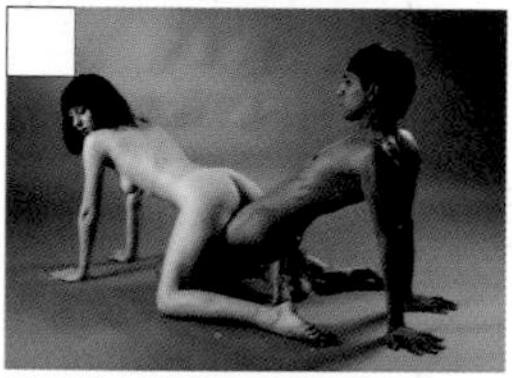
225 The Carriage House

226 Catch You on the Flip Side

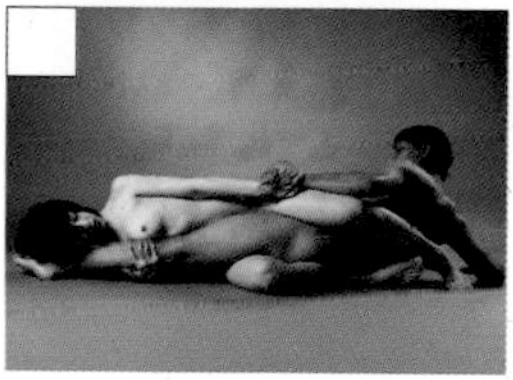
227 The Intertwined Links

228 Chain Me Up

229 Shucking the Oyster

230 Under Wraps

231 The Kitchen Sink

232 Rock-a-Bye Baby

233 The Curling Iron

234 Like a Cat

235 On the Road

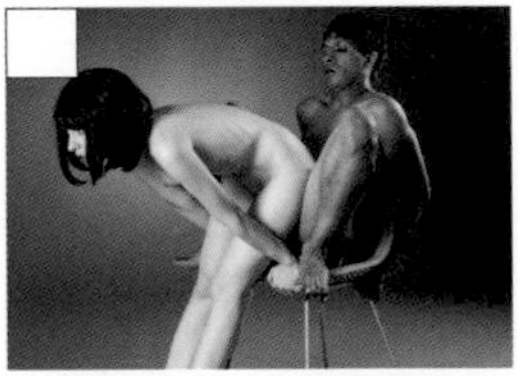

236 The Whoopie Cushion

237 Sailor's Knots

238 The Cancan Dancer

239 The Venus Flytrap

240 The Homestretch

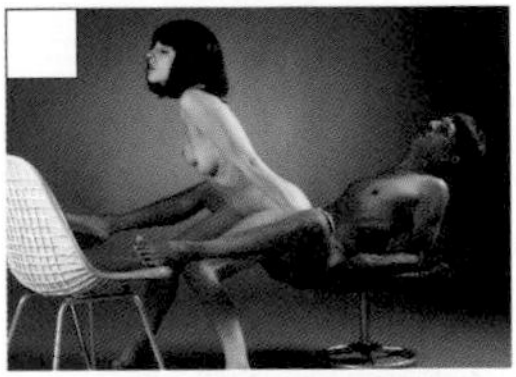

241 The Three-Chair Double Squat

242 Doing Cartwheels